AMAZING MACHINES
BACKHOES

Published by Creative Education and Creative Paperbacks
P.O. Box 227, Mankato, Minnesota 56002
Creative Education and Creative Paperbacks are imprints of
The Creative Company
www.thecreativecompany.us

Design by The Design Lab
Production by Chelsey Luther
Art direction by Rita Marshall
Printed in the United States of America

Photographs by Alamy (Design Pics Inc, GerryRousseau, Napa Valley Register/ZUMA Press Inc), Dreamstime (Chode, Dmitry Kalinovsky, Orangeline, Stefan11, Zilong Li), iStockphoto (gracemom, tinabelle, valio84sl, VILevi)

Library of Congress Cataloging-in-Publication Data
Names: Arnold, Quinn M., author.
Title: Backhoes / Quinn M. Arnold.
Series: Amazing machines.
Includes bibliographical references and index.
Summary: A basic exploration of the parts, variations, and worksites of backhoes, the digging and hauling machines. Also included is a pictorial diagram of variations of backhoes.
Identifiers: ISBN 978-1-60818-885-7 (hardcover) / ISBN 978-1-62832-501-0 (pbk) / ISBN 978-1-56660-937-1 (eBook)
This title has been submitted for CIP processing under LCCN 2017937608.

CCSS: RI.1.1, 2, 4, 5, 6, 7; RI.2.2, 5, 6, 7, 10; RI.3.1, 5, 7, 8; RF.1.1, 3, 4; RF.2.3, 4

First Edition HC 9 8 7 6 5 4 3 2 1
First Edition PBK 9 8 7 6 5 4 3 2 1

Table of Contents

Backhoe Beginnings   4

Backhoe Buckets   7

Compact Backhoes   11

Multipurpose Machines   12

Turning Around   15

Backhoes at Work   16

Amazing Backhoes   20

Backhoe Blueprint   22

Read More   24

Websites   24

Index   24

Backhoes are heavy machines. They dig and load materials. Backhoes were first used in the 1950s. A lot of houses were being built then. Builders needed a machine that could do many jobs.

Reflector strips and flashing lights help backhoes avoid crashes with other big machines.

The loader is usually seven to eight feet (2.1– 2.4 m) wide.

Backhoes have two buckets. The wide bucket on the front of the machine is the loader. It carries dirt, sand, and rocks. A loader fills dump trucks. It can **backfill** holes and plow snow, too.

backfill to refill a hole with the material dug out of it

Made up of a boom and dipper, the excavator arm can move side to side.

The smaller bucket is the excavator. It is one to three feet (0.3–0.9 m) wide. Its teeth sink into hard ground. It digs holes and **trenches**. Stabilizer legs keep the backhoe steady when it is digging.

trenches long, narrow ditches

Compact backhoes are small. They are easier to operate. Compact backhoes are often used to move rocks. Some can dig 10 feet (3 m) deep.

Compact backhoes are popular among farmers and landscapers.

A hammer attachment breaks up hard surfaces like brick or pavement.

A backhoe's buckets can be taken off. Then a big broom, grinder, and pallet fork can be attached. These tools help a backhoe do many different jobs.

grinder a tool that breaks up stumps, rocks, or other materials

pallet fork a two-pronged attachment that lifts and carries pallets

The backhoe operator sits in a chair. The chair faces forward when the loader is working. It turns to the rear to use the excavator. Four tires help a backhoe move around the worksite. The back tires are larger than the front tires.

Backhoes can travel about 25 miles (40.2 km) per hour.

Backhoes often work at construction sites. These heavy machines can help build structures or tear them down. Backhoes work on road construction, too. They can break up old pavement and smooth fresh blacktop.

Most loader buckets have a smooth edge to scoop up material.

Pronged pallet forks make moving heavy loads of lumber fast and easy.

On farms, backhoes may pull up tree stumps or move heavy rocks. Sometimes backhoes dig **foundations**, clear brush, and move trees.

foundations the underground parts of buildings that support the structures

Backhoes are useful heavy machines. You can see them at most worksites. It is fun to watch these heavy machines work!

The sturdy backhoe body and buckets are made of steel.

Backhoe Blueprint

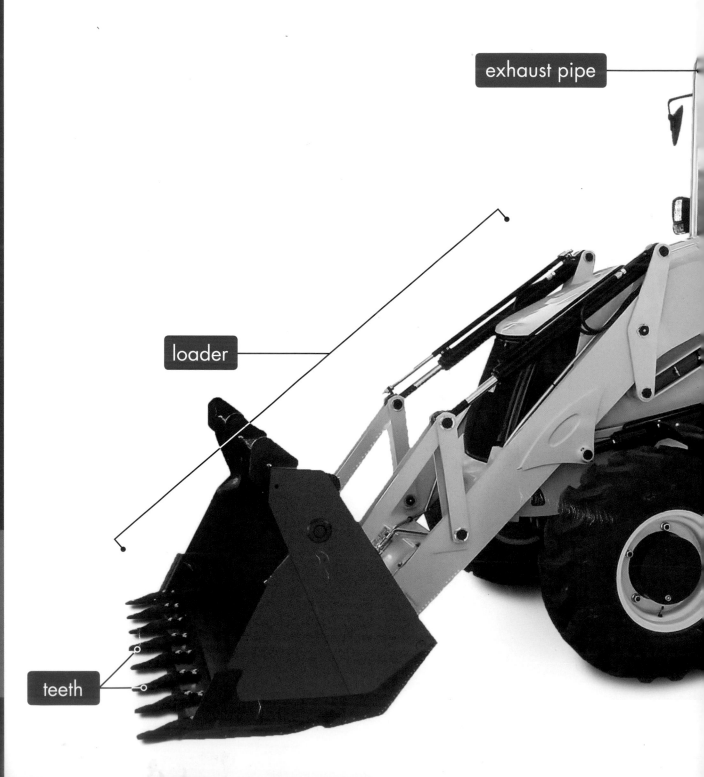

exhaust pipe

loader

teeth

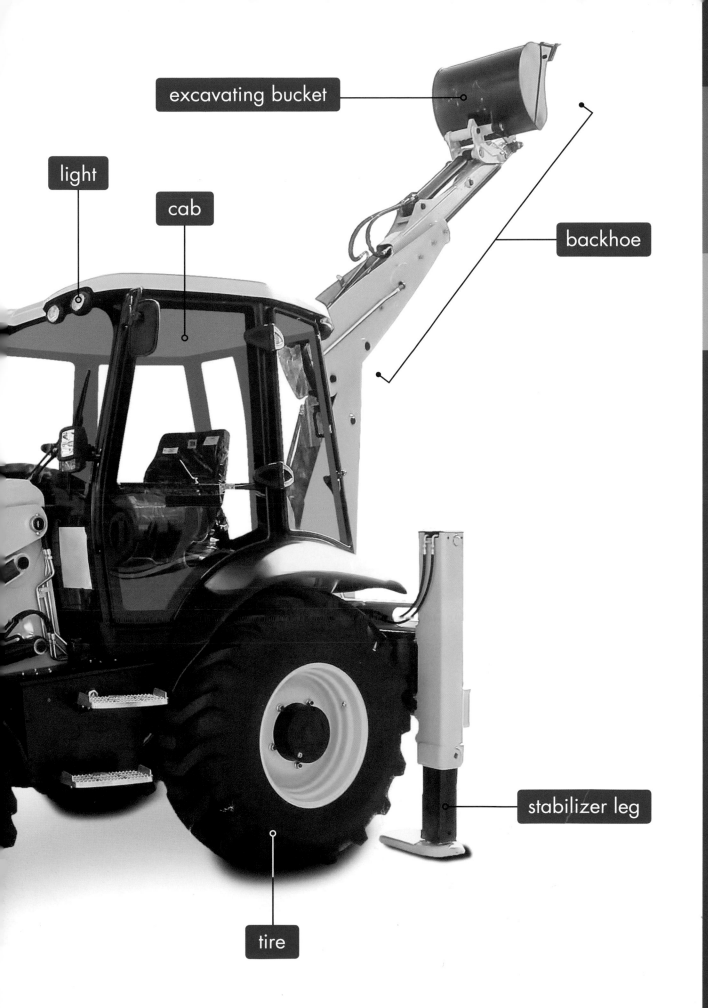

excavating bucket

light

cab

backhoe

stabilizer leg

tire

Read More

Bowman, Chris. *Backhoes*. Minneapolis: Bellwether Media, 2017.

Osier, Dan. *Backhoes*. New York: PowerKids Press, 2014.

Smith, Sian. *Machines on a Construction Site*. Chicago: Heinemann, 2014.

Websites

Backhoe Excavator for Kids: Explore a Backhoe
https://www.youtube.com/watch?v=6D4f6tmmB0s
Watch a video to learn more about backhoes.

Kikki's Workshop
http://www.kenkenkikki.jp/e_index.html
Explore this site to learn more about construction equipment.

Note: Every effort has been made to ensure that the websites listed above are suitable for children, that they have educational value, and that they contain no inappropriate material. However, because of the nature of the Internet, it is impossible to guarantee that these sites will remain active indefinitely or that their contents will not be altered.

Index

attachments 12
compact backhoes 11
construction sites 4, 16
excavator buckets 7, 8, 12, 15, 19
farms 19
loader buckets 7, 15
operators 15
roads 16
stabilizer legs 8
tires 15